LANGUAGE OF LIGHT:

MASTERWORKS FROM THE COLLECTION

GEH

Language of Light: Masterworks from the Collection is dedicated to sharing the rich tradition of the history of photography with the public by serving as a permanent exhibition for the scientific and creative treasures that comprise the Museum's widely acclaimed collections. Common to all museums is the understanding that great collections are primal, poetic resources that provide society with opportunities to expand knowledge, protect one's heritage, inspire creative thinking, and reinforce the value of education. In this particular museum, that awareness is communicated by a special language—the language of light.

Drawing upon the Museum's several collections, which include rare books, artifacts and apparatus, motion picture films, and photographic prints, this exhibition only hints at the great diversity and quality of the hundreds of thousands of objects available for research and enjoyment. While each and every object selected for the collections merits preservation and study, there is always a certain proportion that becomes identified by history as masterworks: photographs that evoke universal aesthetic responses or record the essence of significant moments in time; cameras of such fine design and use of materials that they share the qualities of sculpture; books that change the nature of literature and printed communication; films that enhance and expand one's perception of reality; or

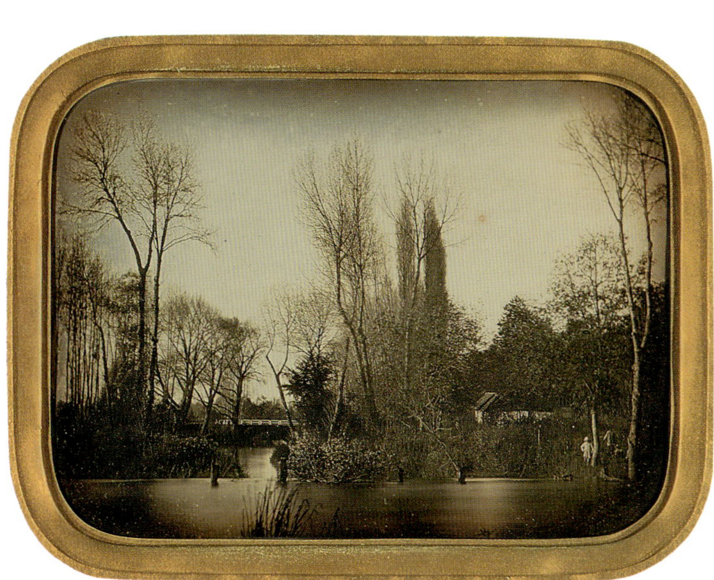

Fig. 1
Alexander-Jean-Pierre Clausel
(French, 1802–1884)
[Landscape, probably
near Troyes, France]
ca. 1855
Whole-plate daguerreotype
Gift of Eastman Kodak
Company, ex-collection
Gabriel Cromer

any of the artifacts and apparatus whose unique invention contributes to a sense of discovery in this ever-changing medium.

There is a fine line to be drawn between masterwork and masterpiece. In the vernacular of contemporary society, the former may be seen as an object of supreme accomplishment, but one among many. The latter has become a means of denoting a hierarchy among objects to satisfy the marketplace. While the objects in this exhibition may be one and the same by definition, it is a passion for quality and the recognition of such that this exhibition is intended to serve.

The opportunity to present such master-works from the Museum's collections in a newly redesigned gallery space could not have taken place without the generosity of the great-grandchildren of Brackett Halford Clark. Their gift has made it possible to rotate selections from the exhibition for the sake of preservation and to publish this booklet, thus acquainting the public with the richness of the Museum's collections. They continue a family tradition that established this gallery in 1963.

I would also like to acknowledge the curatorial staff of the Museum for their expertise and scholarship in organizing the exhibition.

James L. Enyeart

Director

In 1839 the distinguished British scientist Sir John Herschel introduced a neologism to the English language, the word "photography." This new term coupled the Greek word for "light" with the verb "to draw or write." For over a century and a half photography, "writing with light," has been a dominant mode of communication and expression, the quintessential medium of the modern era. Photography and its corollary, the cinematic "moving picture," are mankind's universal language. Like any language, photography has its roots and origins, its evolution, its syntax and grammar, its ever-changing vocabulary, its literature, and its masterworks.

Here is a selection of masterworks written in the language of light. The works were chosen from the millions of objects housed in the International Museum of Photography at George Eastman House. This selection shows the diversity and inventiveness of photographic production, and reflects the special strengths of the Museum's collections of apparatus, images, photographic literature, and movie memorabilia.

The oldest objects on display in this exhibition pre-date the invention of photography. They are optical devices that exploit the phenomenon of persistence of vision to create the illusion of movement. Phenakistoscopes, zoetropes, praxinoscopes, and thaumatropes were among the many early- and mid-nineteenth-century inventions that served both scientific enquiry and popular amusement. The examples of the Plateau Phenakistoscope image discs produced in 1833 (figures 2 and 3) were drawn from the Museum's fine collection of pre-cinema objects. Often the witty, playful frolics of devils and other comic grotesques provided the sequential

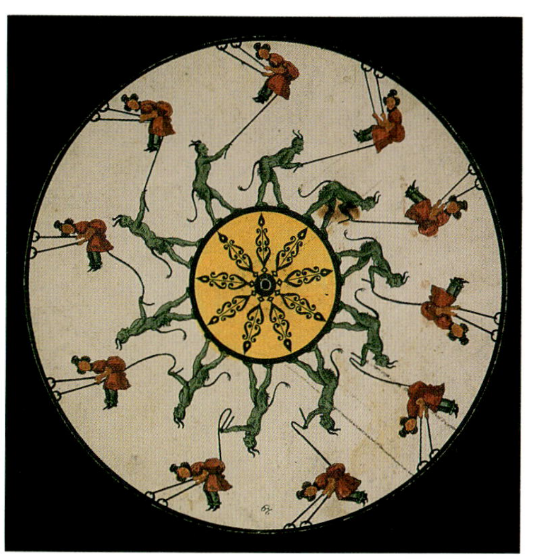 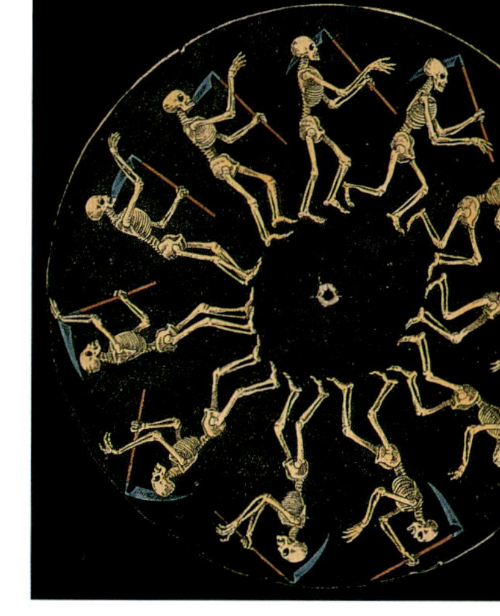

Figs. 2&3
PLATEAU
PHENAKISTOSCOPE
IMAGE DISCS
(France, 1833)
Lithographs with
applied color
Gift of Eastman Kodak
Company, ex-collection
Gabriel Cromer

phases of movement depicted on these image discs. Their motion appeared to be continuous when the discs were spun. From these early efforts, the motion picture evolved.

The daguerreotype, invented by Louis Jacques Mandé Daguerre, was the first practical photographic imaging process to find widespread acceptance. Its diffusion was international, but the art is most closely identified with France, where it originated, and with the United States, where it enjoyed its greatest popularity. Selections from both countries represent the Museum's superb holdings from the daguerreian era. The French landscape tradition is exemplified by Alexandre-Jean-Pierre

Clausel's exquisite view of a river bank in northern France, a masterful rendition of detail and light (figure 1). In contrast to this bucolic scene, the Southworth and Hawes view of the suspension bridge at Niagara Falls represents a visual celebration of American technical achievement (figure 4). It is an unusual outdoor scene from America's most

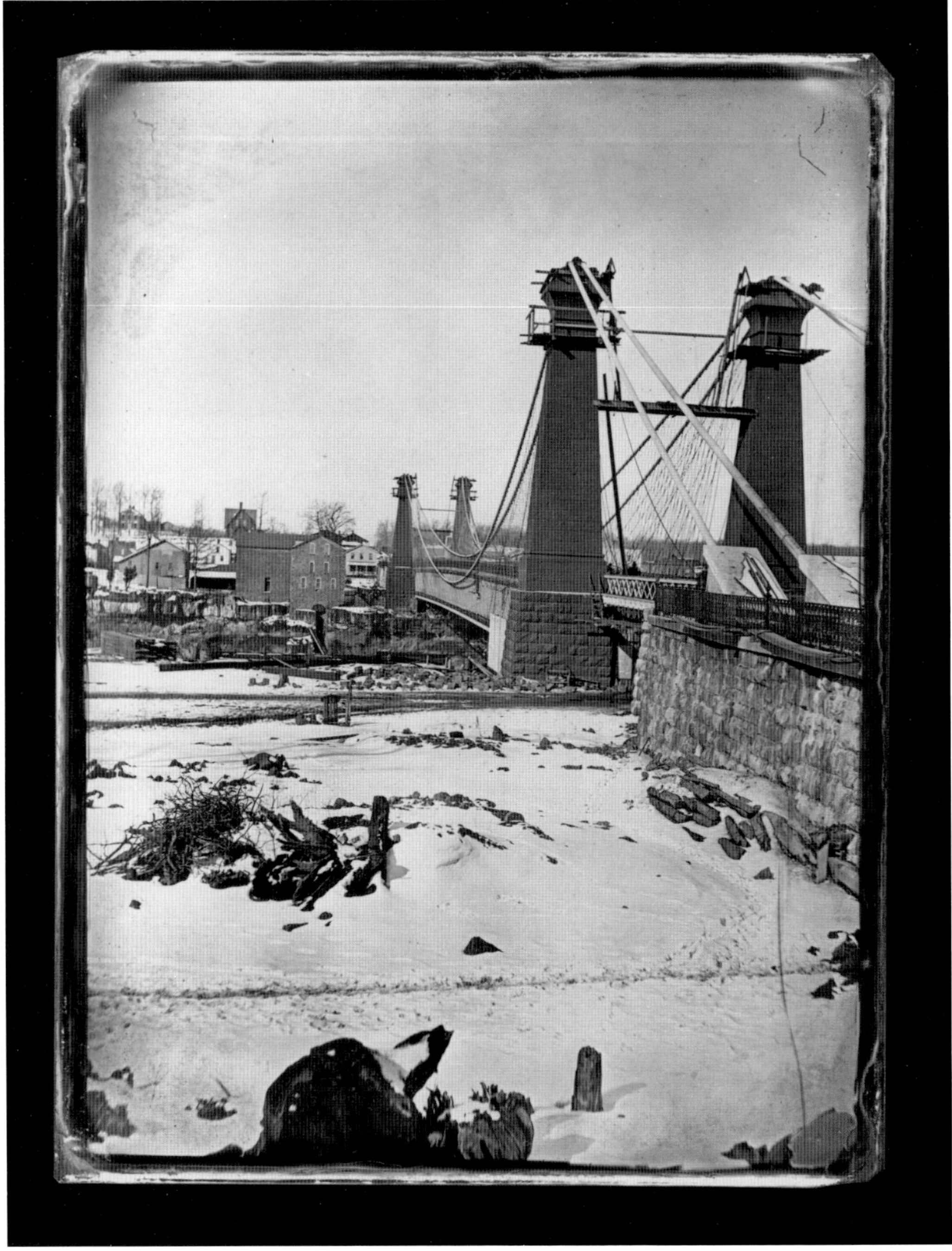

distinguished daguerreotype studio, best known for its superb portrait studies.

The Bemis daguerreotype camera outfit, built in 1840, is a key artifact in the early history of the daguerreian process (figure 5). The fitted wooden trunk containing all the equipment needed to make a full-plate daguerreotype was sold by François Gouraud, Daguerre's first agent in the United States, to Dr. Bemis, a Boston dentist. This outfit, complete with the original bill of sale, provides a unique link between France and America. The camera's country of manufacture is something of a mystery: most probably it was made in France, although the wooden body may have been

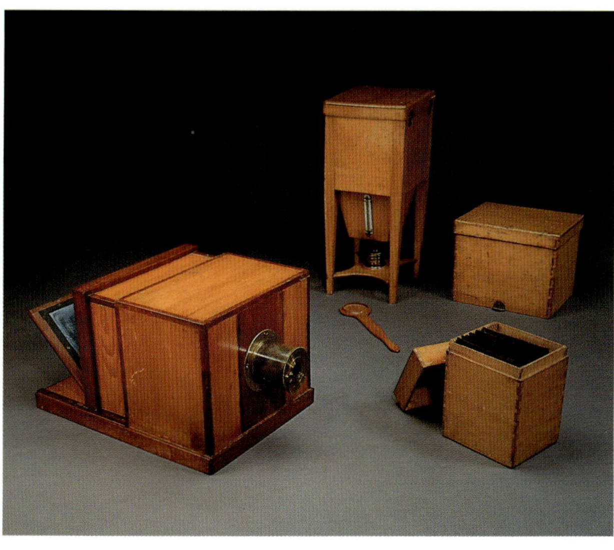

Fig. 5
*BEMIS DAGUERREOTYPE
CAMERA OUTFIT
Attributed to
Alphonse Giroux,
Paris, France
1840
Gift of Eastman Kodak
Company, ex-Eastman
Historical collection*

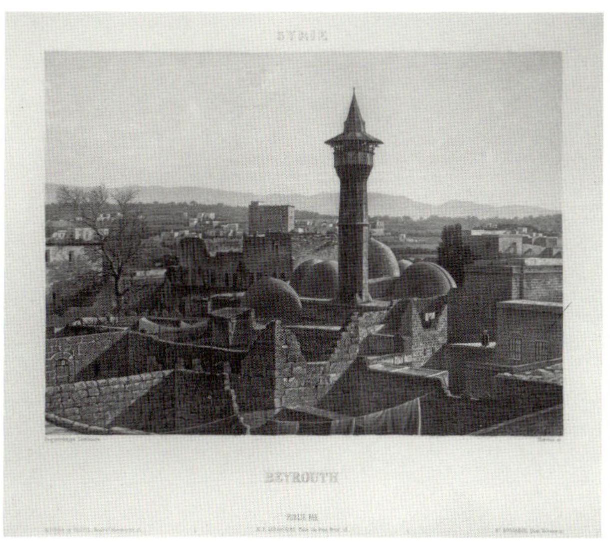

Fig. 6
*After unidentified
photographer
(French?)
SYRIE: BEYROUTH
(SYRIA: BEIRUT)
From:* Excursions
Daguerriennes: Vues et
Monuments les Plus
Remarquables du
Globe *(Commissioned
by Noël Marie Paymal
Lerebours). Paris:
Rittner et Goupil, 1842
Aquatint engraving
by Martens, after
daguerreotype
Gift of Alden Scott Boyer*

fabricated in America and fitted with imported lenses and accessories. Whatever its origin, this is almost certainly the earliest surviving camera to be sold commercially in the United States.

Daguerreotypes, being images formed on sensitized metal plates, could not be published, and yet the illustrated book offered a way of disseminating copies of each precious, unique original. Books of scenic views, with plates engraved by hand after original daguerreotypes, inhabit that middle ground between photographic exactitude and the handwork of the graphic artist working in the older tradition of the topographic print. Nowhere is this better seen than in *Excursions Daguerriennes*, one of the great triumphs of French photographic publishing (see figure 6). *Excursions* was the creation of the optician and entrepreneur Lerebours, who, in the early days of the daguerreotype, commissioned some of the best practitioners of the new art to capture "the most remarkable views and monuments of the world," and then selected 111 fine views of the most picturesque aspects of Europe and the East. It is a true *livre de luxe:* the list of subscribers is headed by the King of France.

The Museum's fine holdings of early paper photography include 440 salted paper prints created between 1843 and 1847 by David Octavius Hill and Robert Adamson of Edinburgh, Scotland. In the five short years of their collaboration, Hill and Adamson produced the first large, coherent body of aesthetically significant work in the history of photography. The arrangement of members of the Watson and Milne families (see cover photograph) is one of their extraordinary group portraits in the tradition of the conversation piece, where individual character is expressed, while attitudes, glances, and gestures unite the figures in a harmonious composition that fully exploits the bold chiaroscuro contrasts of light and shadow that characterize the calotype process.

The advent of photography on paper opened up the possibilities for book illustration using original prints, pasted onto the page. One of the most magnificent of these early illustrated books, the *Reports by the Juries*, documents that defining event of mid-century Victorian England, the Great Exhibition of the Works of Industry of All Nations, which took place at the Crystal Palace. The four volumes of the Jury Reports were bound in red morocco leather, with the intertwined initials of Victoria and Albert stamped in gold upon the cover (figure 7). Hundreds of objects of human ingenuity and craft, the finest

Fig. 7
Rivière Bindery
(British, 1829–1939)
BINDING
From: Great Exhibition
of the Works of Industry
of All Nations, 1851.
Reports by the Juries...
London: Spicer
Brothers, 1852.
Presentation copy
from Her Majesty's
Commissioners to
Arthur Kett Barclay

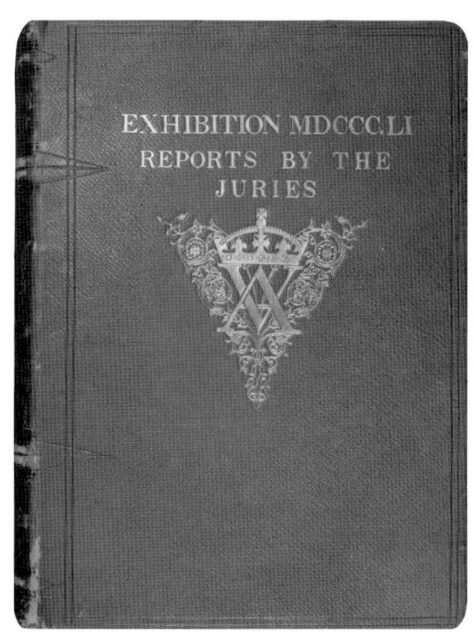

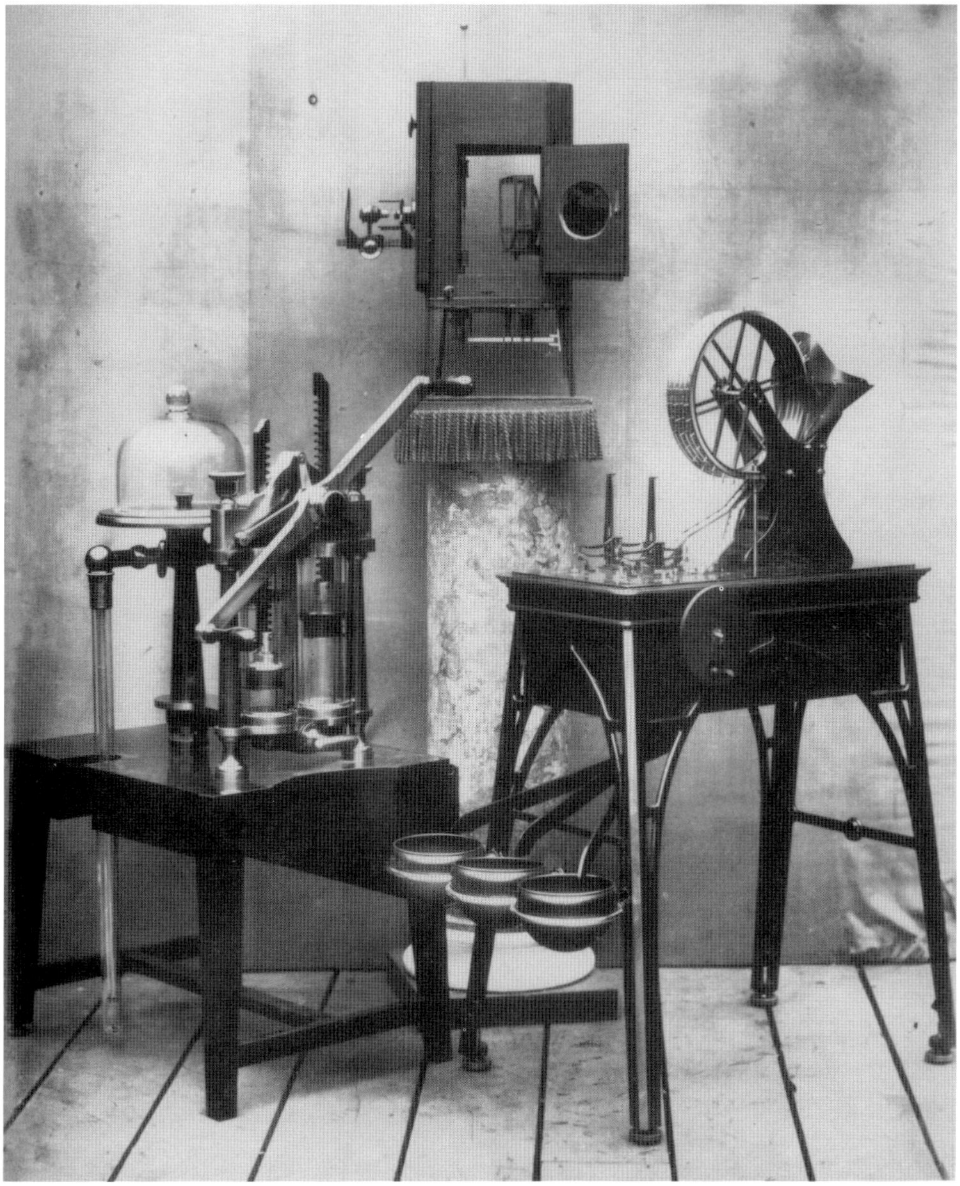

Fig. 8
Hugh Owen or
C. M. Ferrier
(English, 1804–1881
and French, 1811–1889)
PHILOSOPHICAL
INSTRUMENTS
From: Great Exhibition
of the Works of Industry
of All Nations, 1851.
Reports by the Juries...
Salted paper print

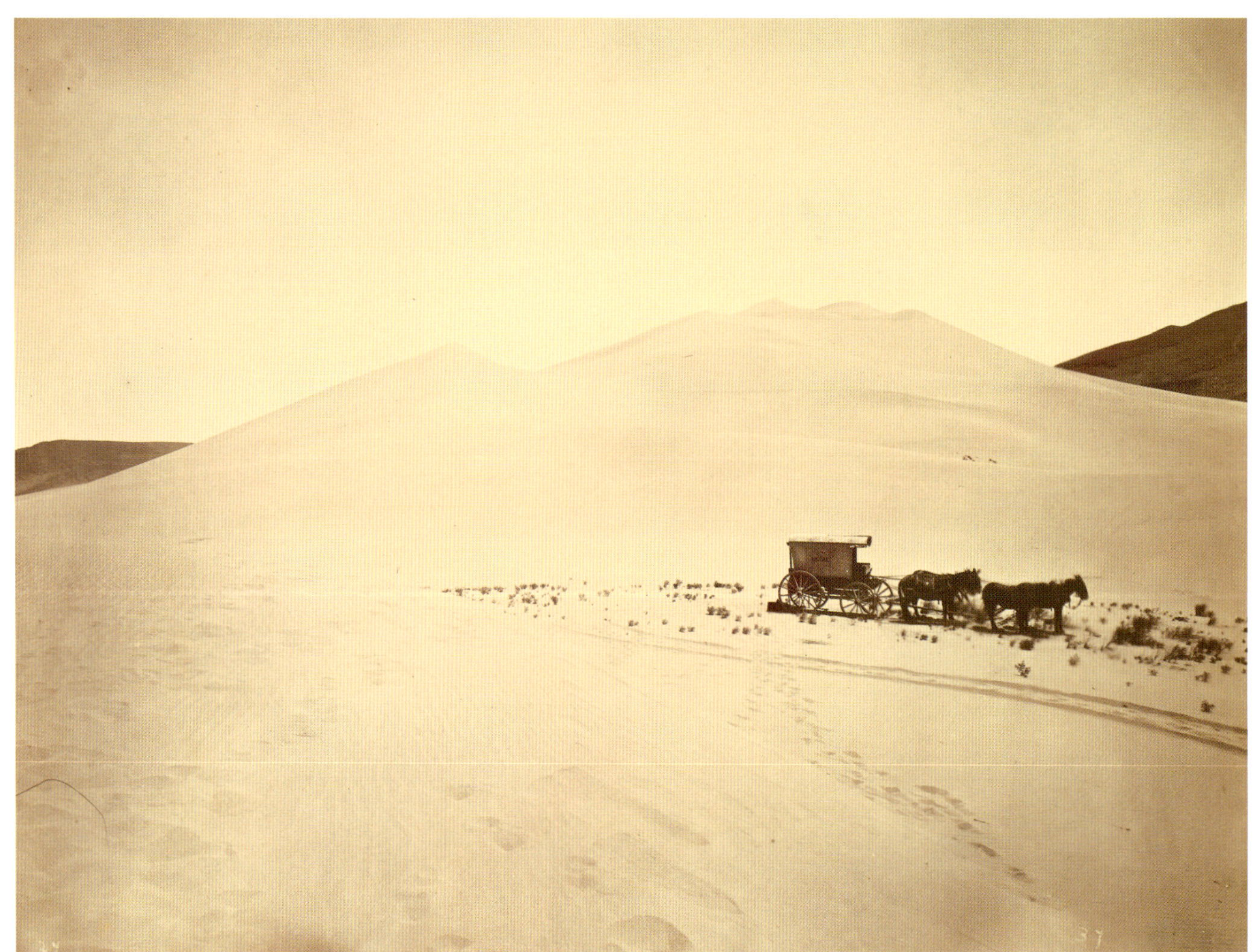

Fig. 9
Timothy O'Sullivan
(American, 1840–1882)
*SAND DUNES NEAR
SAND SPRINGS, NEVADA*
1867
Albumen print
Gift of Harvard University

inventions of the Industrial Revolution and the spoils of empire, are recorded in the salted paper prints that illustrate this sumptuous book (see figure 8). The work is an interesting transitional piece in the history of photography, for most of the illustrations were printed from paper negatives, but a few were made from a new (and short-lived) process, the albumen-coated glass-plate negative.

By the mid-1850s, the clarity of the negatives produced by the wet-collodion process had rendered all earlier photographic processes obsolete. In spite of its clumsiness, the wet collodion negative and the albumen print dominated photography in the studio and in the field for the next thirty years.

While field photography had been widely practiced in Europe since the late 1840s, it was virtually unknown in America before 1860. Timothy O'Sullivan mastered the use of the wet-plate camera in the field during the American Civil War. Afterwards, as a civilian employee of the Army, he worked as one of the most notable expeditionary photographers of the American West. Hauling his heavy equipment through the dunes near Sand Springs, Nevada, O'Sullivan captured the image of his photographic wagon standing in the middle ground, alone in the immensity of the desert landscape (figure 9).

Two contrasting approaches to portraiture may be seen in the contemporaneous work of

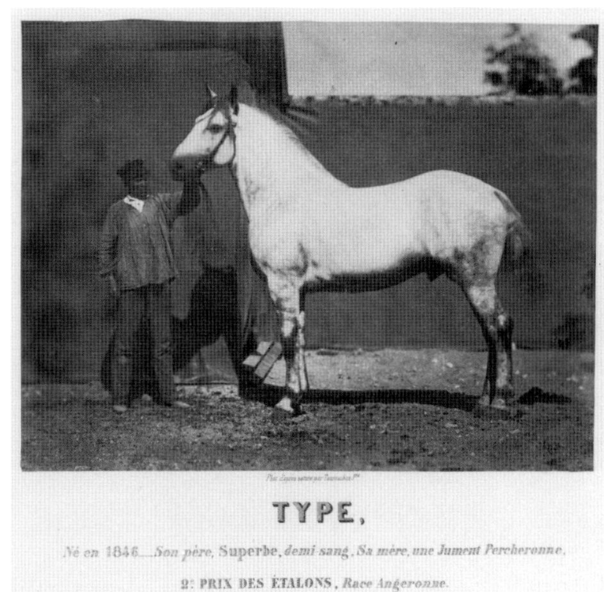

Fig. 10
Adrien Tournachon
(French, 1825–1903)
TYPE
1855
From album:
Races Chevaline
& Asine, Primès a
L'Exposition de 1855
Albumen print

A. A. E. Disdéri and Julia Margaret Cameron
(figures 11 and 12). Disdéri's fashionable Parisian
studio specialized in the celebrities of the Second
Empire. Disdéri did much to promulgate the
modern cult of the celebrity by introducing the
carte-de-visite, small-format images that quickly
became the rage and were collected in quantity.
An uncut carte-de-visite sheet shows how multiple
images were turned out for mass distribution. In
contrast, the portraits created by Cameron were
personal artistic statements, idealizing visions of
friends and family, often in allegorical guise. One
of her most expressive portraits is the profile study of
her niece, Mrs. Herbert Duckworth. This masterpiece
shows Cameron's unorthodox and characteristic use
of focus, and the effect she achieved by deliberately
throwing the image slightly out of focus.

The wet-plate process imposed severe
restrictions on camera design, since the sensitized
materials dripped corrosive chemicals, which inevit-
ably caused severe damage. Cameras had to be
simple and rugged. A charming exception was the

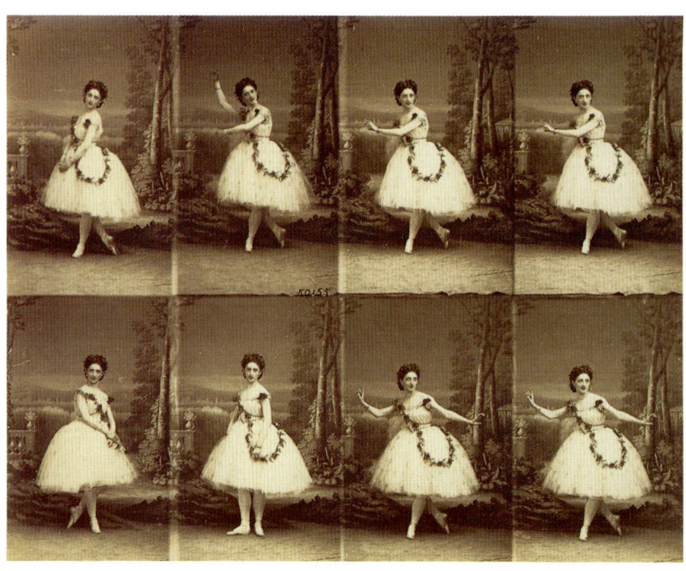

Fig. 11
André-Adolphe-Eugène
Disdéri
(French, 1819–1889)
[Martha Muraviena
in the ballet Nemea]
1864
Albumen print, uncut
carte-de-visite sheet

Fig. 12
Julia Margaret Cameron
(British, 1815–1879)
MRS. HERBERT DUCKWORTH
AS JULIA JACKSON
ca. 1867
Albumen print
Gift of Alden Scott Boyer

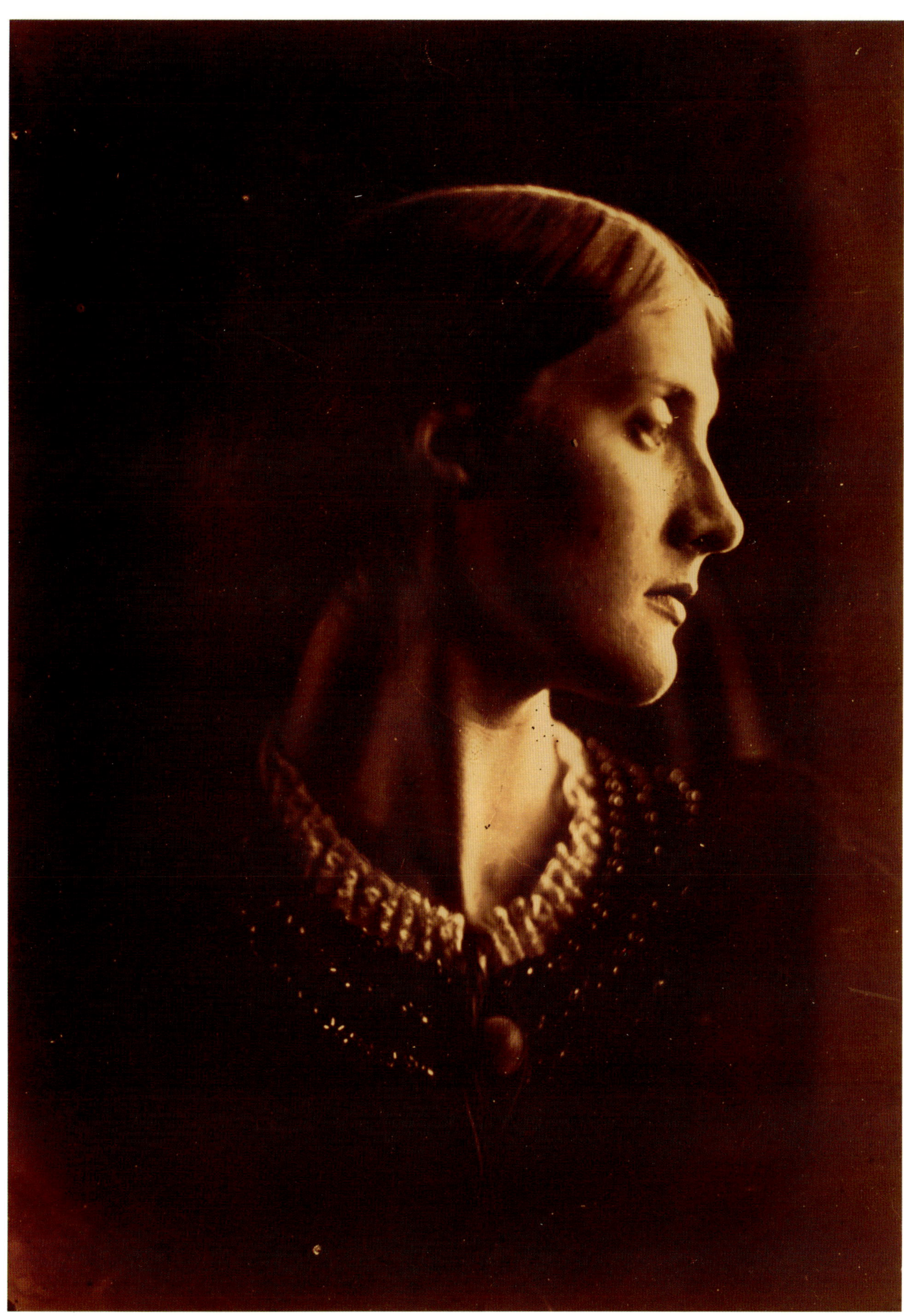

Chambre Automatique de Bertsch, the world's first sub-miniature camera. The jewel-like elegance of this little machine anticipates later camera design. The Museum owns a complete outfit, with fitted box containing the camera, uncoated plates, and all of the chemicals needed to make a wet-plate negative (figure 13).

Another exceptional design from this era was the Dubroni (figure 14). It is frequently (but not quite accurately) called the first instant camera, since all processing could be contained within the

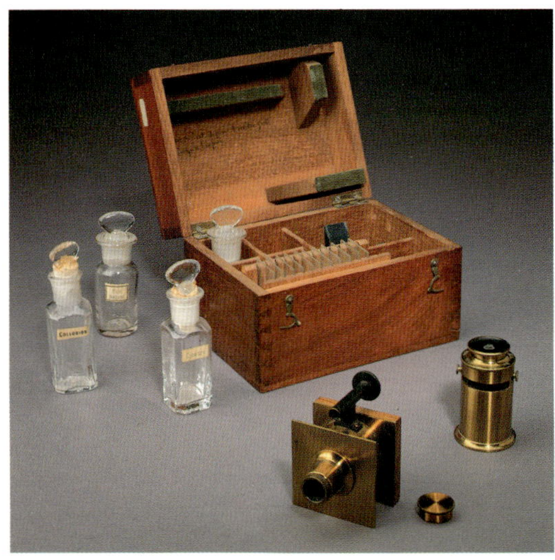

Fig. 13
CHAMBRE AUTOMA-
TIQUE DE BERTSCH
Adolphe Bertsch,
Paris, France
ca. 1861
Gift of Eastman Kodak
Company, ex-collection
Gabriel Cromer

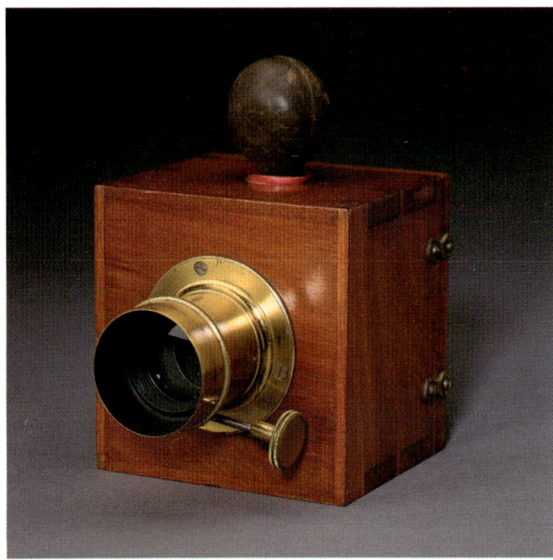

Fig. 14
DUBRONI
Maison Dubroni,
Paris, France
1865
Gift of Eastman Kodak
Company, ex-collection
Gabriel Cromer

Fig. 15
Austin A. Turner
(American, 1831–1866)
RESIDENCE OF
F. A. THOMPSON.
TUBBY HOOK
From: Villas on the
Hudson. A Collection
of Photo-Lithographs
of Thirty-One Country
Residences. *New York:*
D. Appleton & Company,
1860
Photolithographic print

camera body. The central portion of the Dubroni was made of glass or ceramic. A wet plate could be sensitized, developed, and fixed by introducing chemicals into this chamber through a tiny hole at the top. The finished negative was then removed and washed. This eliminated the need for a darkroom in the field, normally a prerequisite of wet-plate photography. The Dubroni was made by Bourdin, a distinguished French manufacturer of photographic equipment, who used an anagram of his name to avoid confusion with his firm's standard products.

Although the albumen print dominated photographic production in the 1860s and '70s, many photomechanical processes were also utilized in the attempt to produce, at a reasonable cost, permanent, non-fading multiple copies that faithfully translated the photographic image into printers' ink. Two examples are seen in *Villas on the Hudson*, which employed the difficult and short-lived photolithographic process (figure 15), and Thomas Annan's *Photographs of the Old Closes and Streets of Glasgow* (figure 16), printed in one of the most

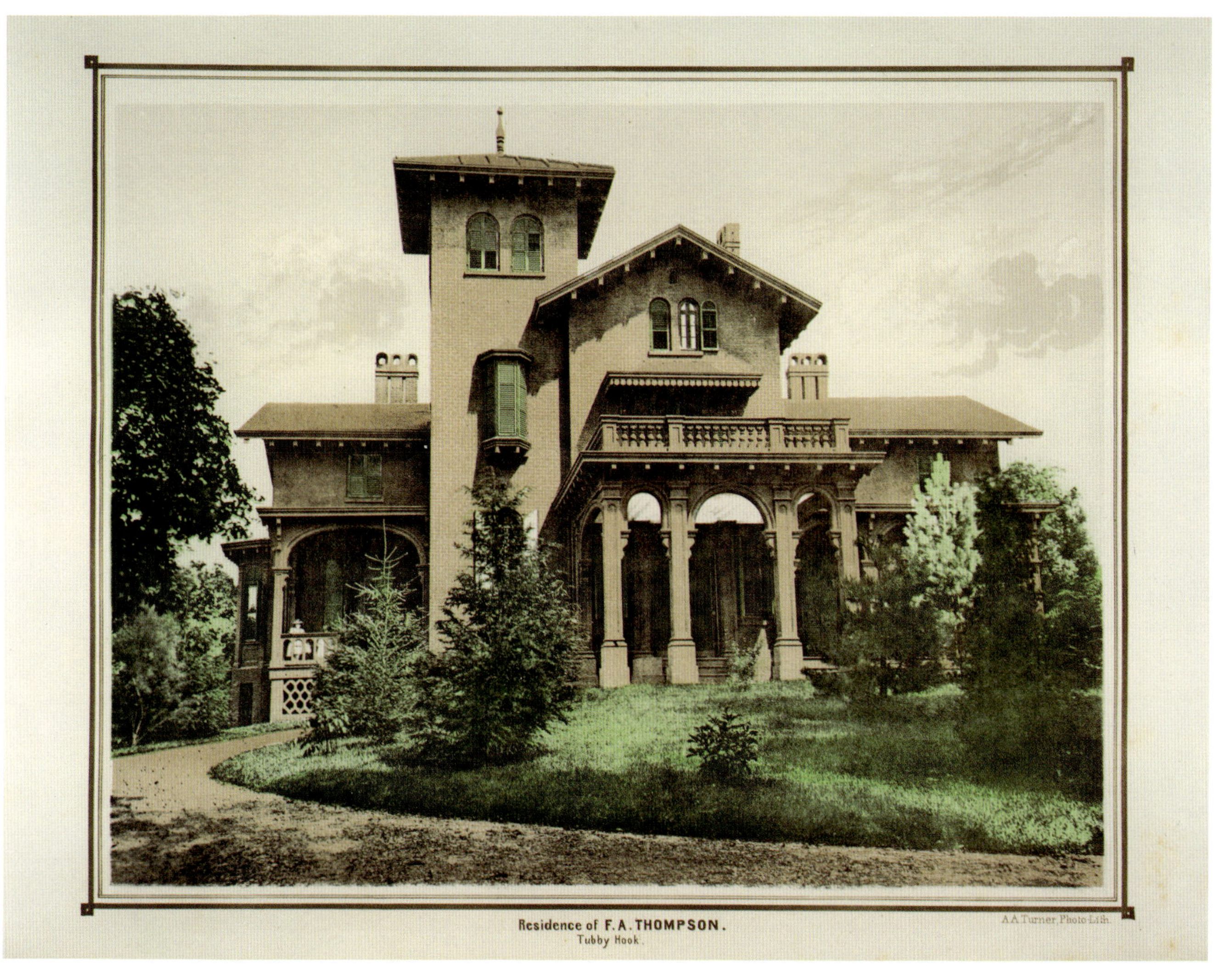

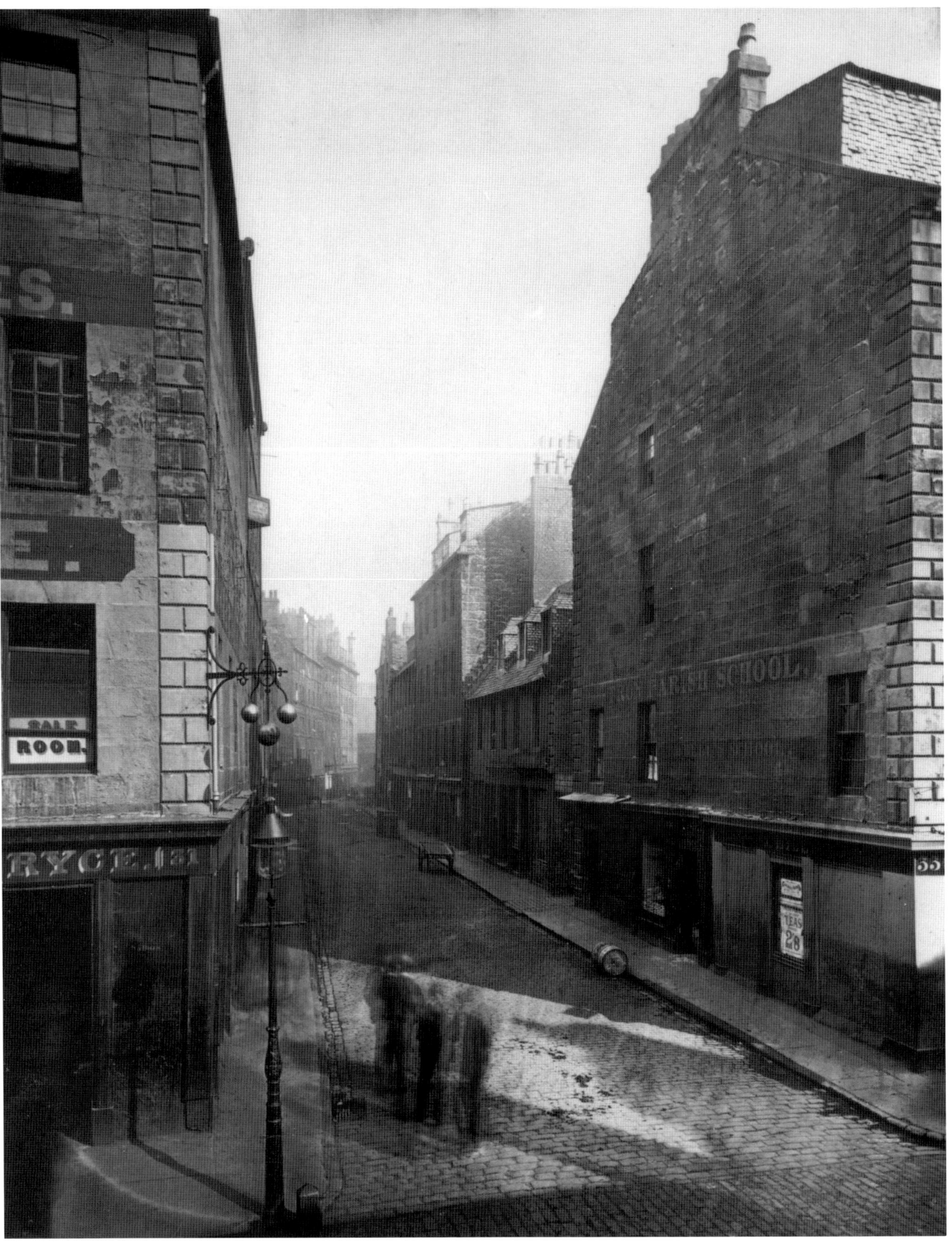

S.
SALE
ROOM.
RYCE.
PARISH SCHOOL
55
TEAS
28

Fig. 16
Thomas Annan
(Scottish, 1829–1887)
PRINCES STREET,
FROM KING STREET
ca. 1868
From portfolio:
Photographs of the
Old Closes and Streets
of Glasgow, 1866/1877.
Glasgow, Scotland:
Glasgow City
Improvement Trust,
1878, plate 24
Carbon print

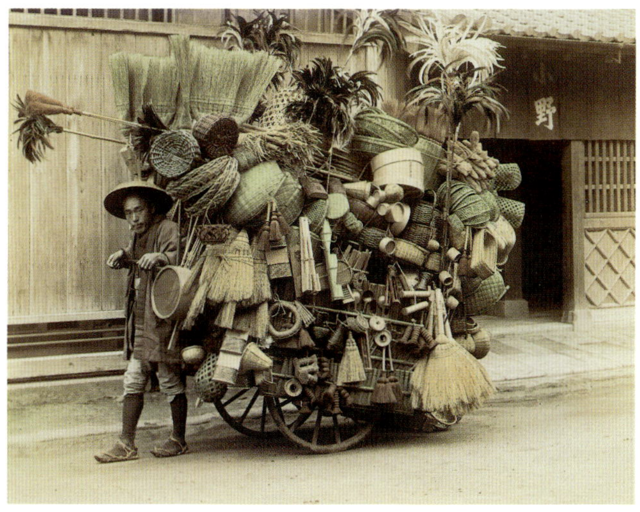

Fig. 17
Unidentified photographer
(Japanese)
AN ITINERANT
MERCHANT
From: Frank Brinkley, ed.,
Japan: Described and
Illustrated by the
Japanese. *Mikado edition.*
Boston: J. B. Millet,
1897–1898. No. 18
of 250 copies
Hand-colored
albumen print
Gift of the University
of Rochester Library

satisfactory and widely used photomechanical processes, the carbon print, known for its permanency. The two books form an interesting comparison.

A. A. Turner's *Villas on the Hudson,* published in 1860, is the first major American illustrated book to employ photolithography. The expert application of three separate colors by stenciling enhances the charm of this compendium of tasteful domestic architecture, showcasing the residences of wealthy and successful antebellum New Yorkers. Annan's work memorializes a very different sort of dwelling, the crowded tenements of the Old City of Glasgow, which by mid-century had become one of the most horrendous slums of Europe. Just before the area was razed in an early civic urban renewal project, the city administration commissioned Thomas Annan, a commercial photographer and a specialist in carbon printing, to record the appearance of this historic quarter. In fulfilling his commission Annan created the first systematic documentation of a modern urban slum. *Old Closes* is now recognized as one of the essential portrayals of the dark side of the Victorian age.

As photographic technology evolved and gelatin dry plates replaced the difficult wet-plate process, camera designers gained a new freedom to create cameras that were simple, compact, and inexpensive. Novel and eccentric designs were also possible. The shape of the Escopette (figure 18)

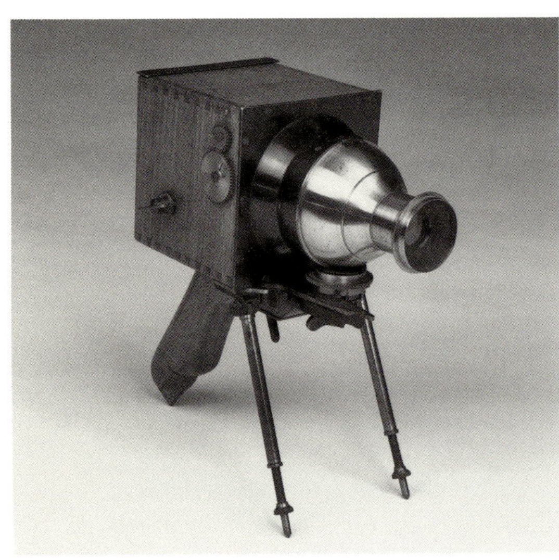

Fig. 18
THE ESCOPETTE
E.V. Boissonas, SA,
Geneva, Switzerland
1888
Gift of Eastman Kodak
Company, ex-collection
Gabriel Cromer

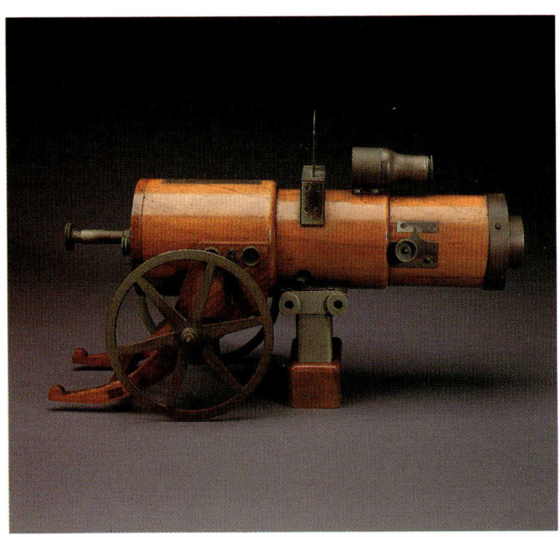

Fig. 19
RÄDERKANONE
(WHEELED CANNON
CAMERA)
Romaine Talbot,
Berlin, Germany
1912
Gift of Kodak Pathé

suggested an antique musket, although this Swiss camera of 1888 was technologically advanced, being the first European camera to use George Eastman's new flexible film. Another "firearm" was designed by the German manufacturer Romaine Talbot in 1912. His Räderkanone or "wheeled cannon" (figure 19) used ferrotype dry plates, which could be developed immediately in a small tank positioned underneath the barrel of the "cannon." Talbot probably intended these novel cameras to be used by street photographers taking pictures of children.

By the turn of the century, the introduction of mass-produced films and printing papers and practical photomechanical reproduction techniques had transformed photography, making it truly a mass-medium and bringing new aesthetic challenges. One important response was to choose subjects, compositional devices, and specialized printing mediums that associated photography with more traditional forms of the visual arts. Edward Steichen, an artist well represented in the Museum's collection, was one of the masters of the pictorialist movement. His youthful "Self-portrait" (figure 20), a gravure reproduced from a negative of his original gum print and published in the April 1903 issue of the magazine *Camera Work*, exemplifies this approach to photography.

By the teens, even the leaders of pictorialism were exploring new techniques that consciously

Fig. 20
Edward Steichen
(American, b. Luxembourg,
1879–1973)
SELF-PORTRAIT
1901
From: Camera Work,
no. 2, April 1903
Photogravure

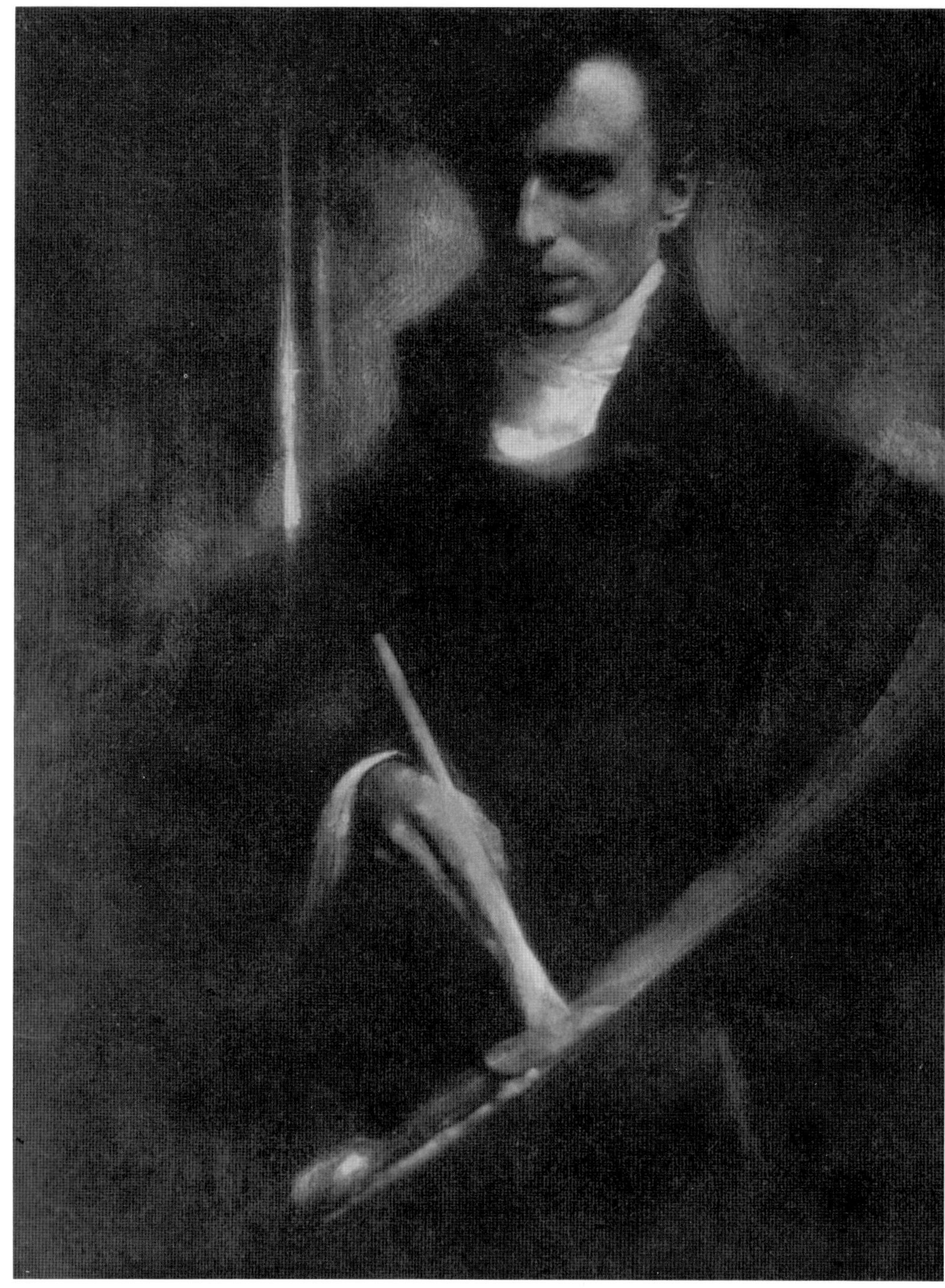

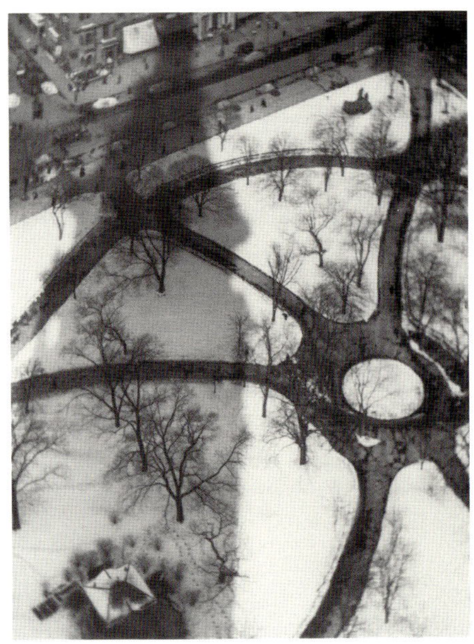

exploited the unique qualities of the camera's vision. Alvin Langdon Coburn's "Octopus" of 1912 (figure 21) is a deliberately achieved in-camera abstraction that anticipates the revolutionary use of perspective and viewpoint by the European avant-garde of the 1920s. Edward Steichen's "Isadora Duncan at the Portal of the Parthenon" (figure 22), presages this artist's shift towards a technically purer vision. The modernists' desire to distill abstract form from nature and to express the sensuous, tactile qualities of surface through the exquisitely crafted

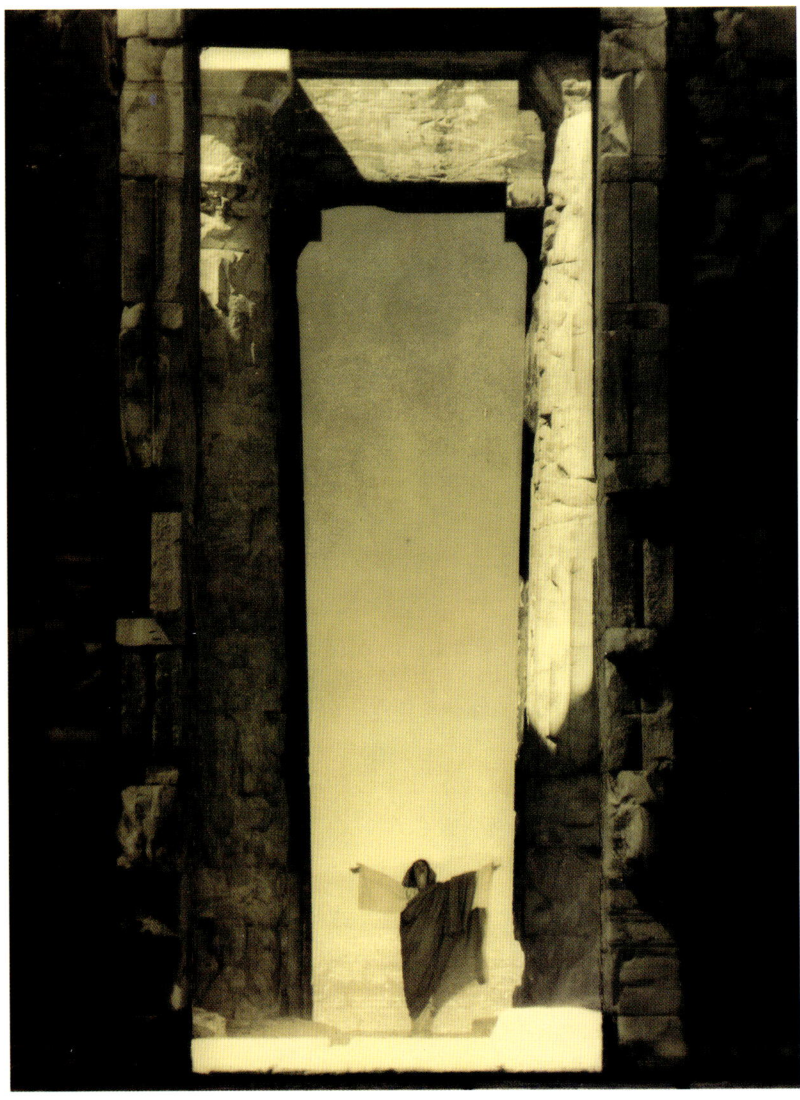

print is shown in Imogen Cunningham's "Calla" (figure 23).

A century of cinema's history is preserved in the Museum's film collection, which is especially strong in classic American films from the silent and sound periods, German and French films of the nitrate era (pre-1950), and independent documentary and avant-garde films. The history of moving images is constituted not only by the motion picture itself, but also by those other products of film culture, the high-gloss photographic star portrait, lithographic film posters, film stills, movie scripts and music cue sheets, cinema lobby cards and similar pieces of movie memorabilia, all housed in the collection of the Film Department.

Soon after the birth of cinema, the nascent American film industry realized that the success of motion pictures was dependent on a well-oiled publicity machine. As a result, film companies set up publicity offices, which churned out a steady stream of images to advertise their films. Situated between commerce and artifice, these objects were

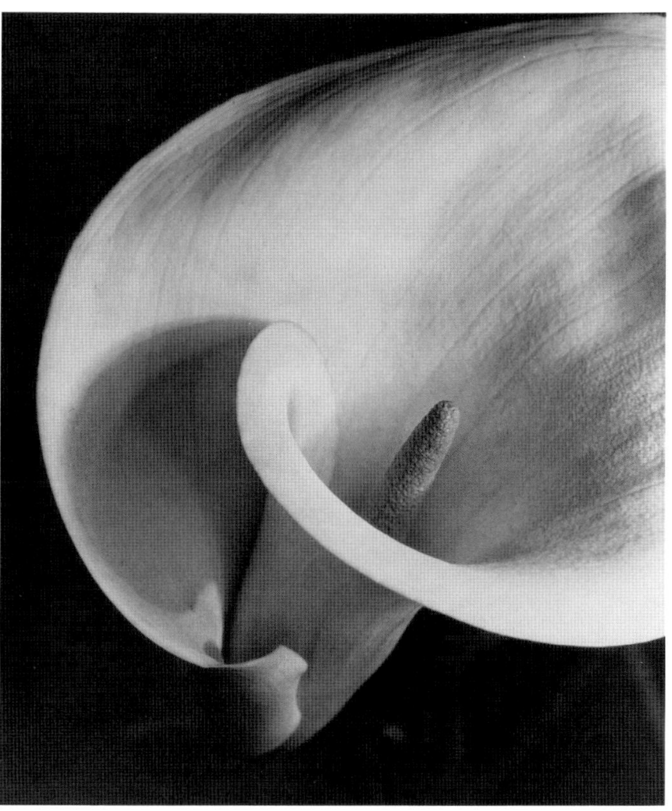

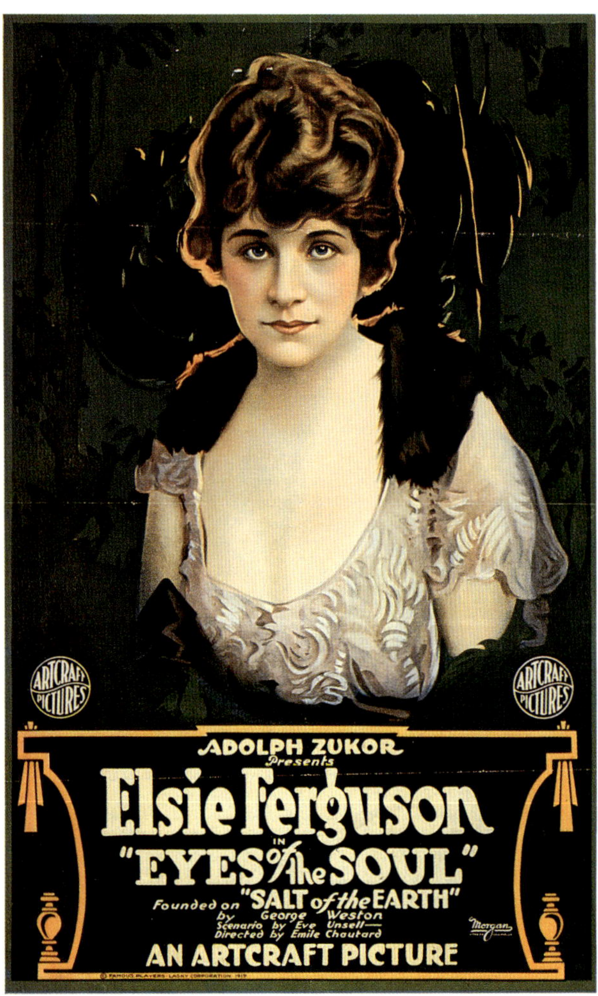

Fig. 24
EYES OF THE SOUL
Famous Players-
Lasky Corp.
(USA, 1921)
Motion picture poster
Offset color lithograph

often of striking beauty. An exquisite example of the high quality of American film poster art is the offset color lithograph from 1921 portraying Elsie Ferguson, star of EYES OF THE SOUL (figure 24). With its frontal view of the actress, her eyes directly engaging the viewer, this image is the perfect visualization of the film's title.

The Museum owns a major collection of German and Soviet film posters. A rare Soviet poster from 1939 (figure 25) advertises LENIN IN 1918, a propagandistic biography. Employing the officially sanctioned style of Socialist Realism, the poster depicts Lenin as a father-figure, the benevolent patriarch of the nation, guiding the education of his children. Here the bold graphic style of the advertisement serves an ideological purpose far different from Hollywood's industry of entertainment.

Another way the motion picture studios advertised films was through star portraits, produced primarily for distribution to the fan magazines. These pictures were meant to create myths, to exude glamour, to be larger than life. A perfect case in point is the portrait of Louise Brooks (figure 26), made in 1929 by the Studio Lorelle in Paris. With her pageboy haircut and her innocent yet beguiling smile, the American actress was regarded by the Parisian public of the late 1920s as an icon of modernity, the quintessential flapper, a liberated woman who demanded her sexual freedom.

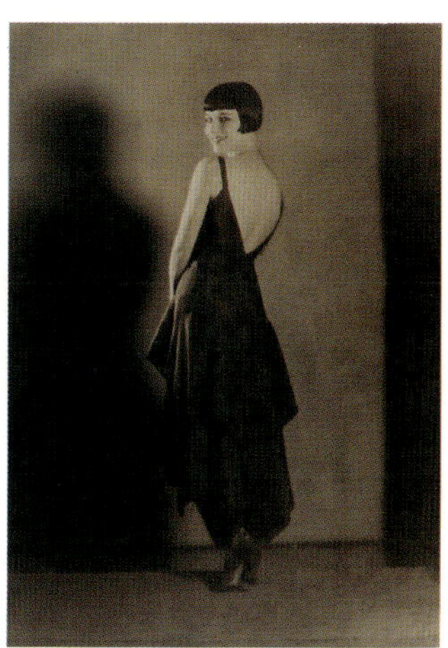

Fig. 26
LOUISE BROOKS
1929
Promotional portrait for
PRIX DE BEAUTE
(France, 1929)
Gelatin silver print
Gift of Louise Brooks

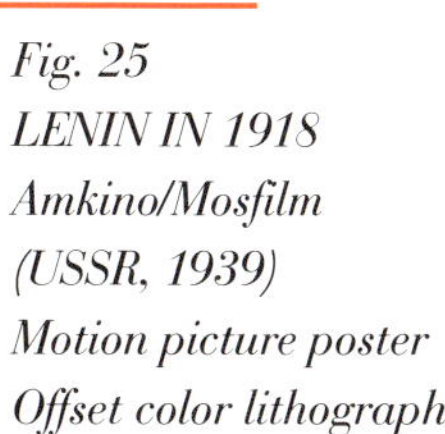

Fig. 25
LENIN IN 1918
Amkino/Mosfilm
(USSR, 1939)
Motion picture poster
Offset color lithograph

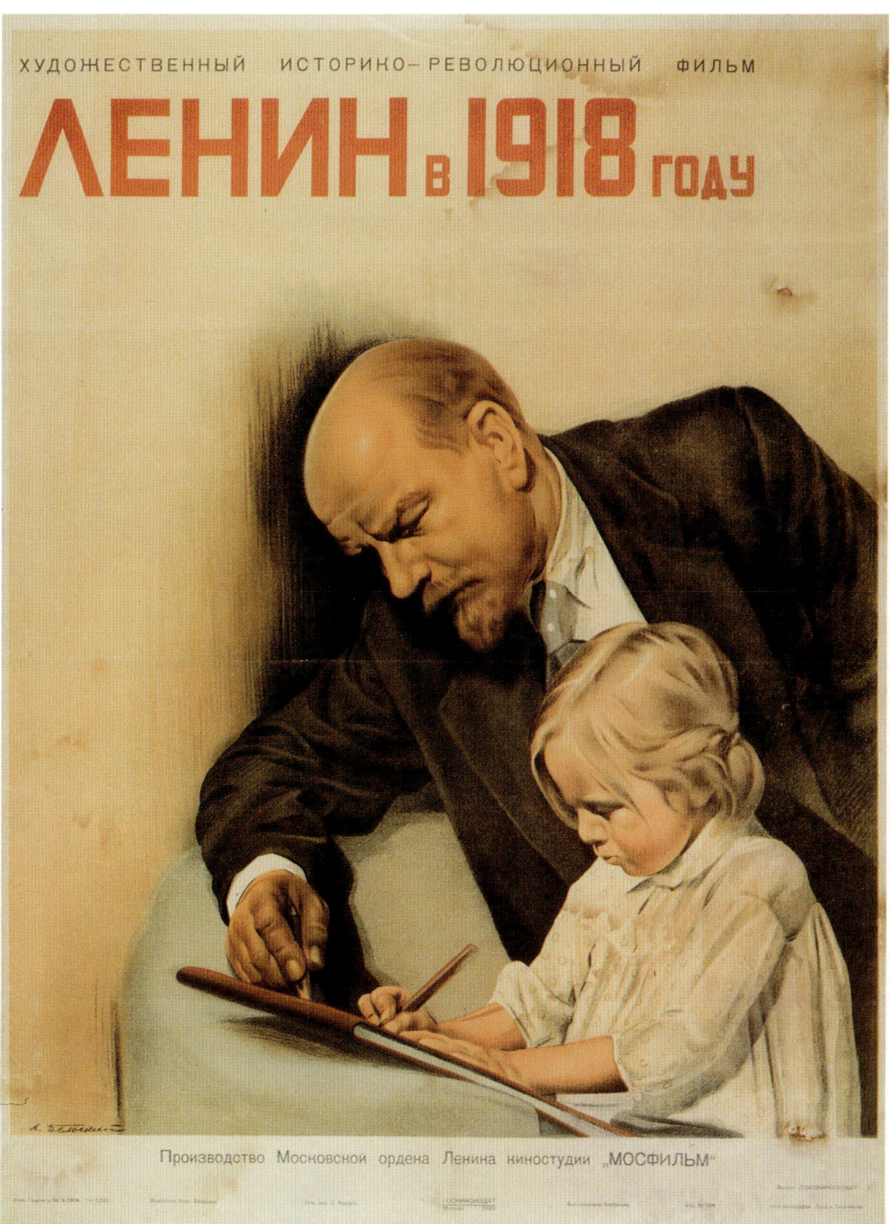

The Modernist movement acknowledged the innovations of cinema. This new, experimental aesthetic explored the capabilities of the mechanical "camera eye" to create a style appropriate to the machine age. The German avant-garde of the 1920s played a key role in Modernism's evolution. László Moholy-Nagy, the iconoclastic new instructor at the Bauhaus design school, issued the radical manifesto for this movement in his 1925 publication *Malerei, Photographie, Film*. Moholy-Nagy advocated the "new vision" with its radically tilted perspectives, and the construction of images by optical and technical means.

Among the new techniques espoused was the use of photo-collage. Moholy-Nagy was a master of this form. Photo-collage allowed absolute creative control over all the elements in the composition: its pictorial contents, its structural pattern, and the articulation of space within the image. The result is seen in "Massenpsychose" (Mass Psychosis) (figure 27), in which the artist comments upon the contemporary political and psychological climate of Weimar Germany.

Aleksander Rodschenko's collaboration with the poet Mayakovski brought the tenets of Russian constructivism to the newly created form of photomontage in images that capture the spirit and energy of the jazz age (figure 28). Photomontage became a political weapon in the hands of John Heartfield, who illustrated Tucholsky's biting satire of Weimar Germany. The shouting man on the cover of *Deutschland, Deutschland Über Alles* (figure 29) wears a combination of top hat and Prussian helmet, the headgear of the military-industrial complex.

As the twentieth century progressed, the increasing availability of smaller cameras and fast

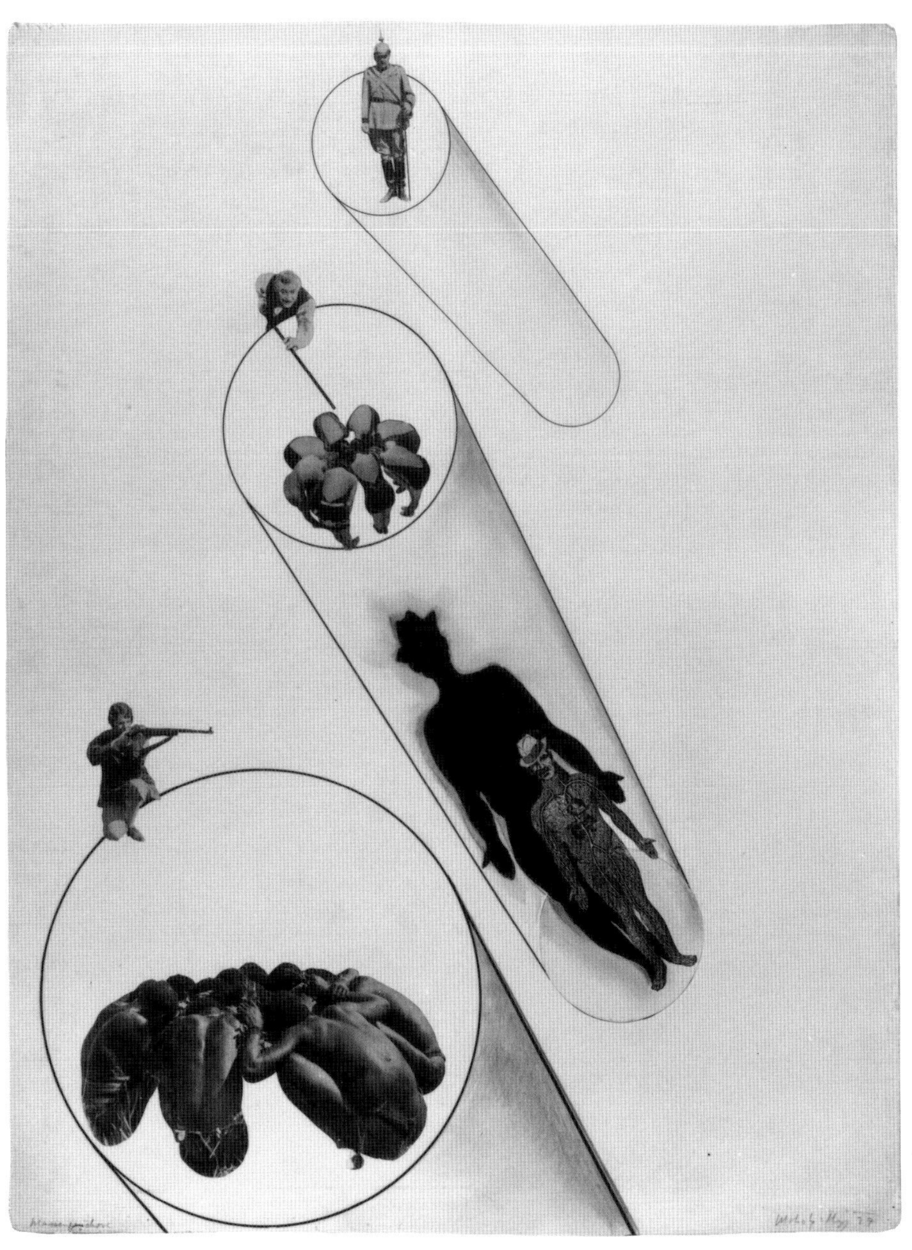

films encouraged new approaches to photography.
Helen Levitt was one of the pioneer American street
photographers of the 1940s, using her camera
spontaneously to isolate and document moments
of everyday life that define the nature of human
relationships (figure 30). This humanistic vision also
informs the work of Robert Frank, whose journey
across America in 1955–56 yielded "Trolley, New
Orleans" (figure 31). Frank, a Swiss photographer

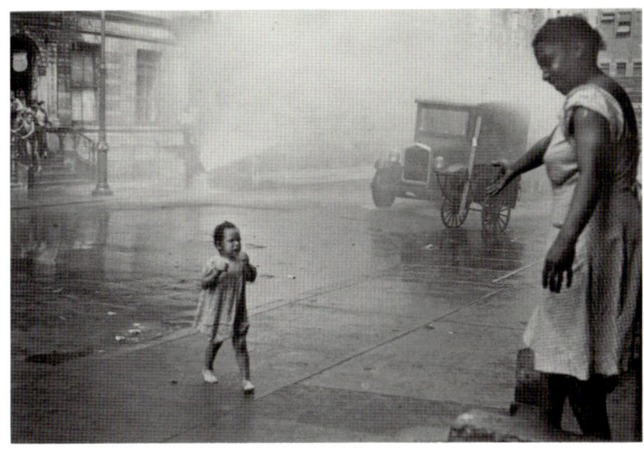

Fig. 30
Helen Levitt
(American, b. 1918)
EAST HARLEM
ca. 1947
Gelatin silver print
© Helen Levitt

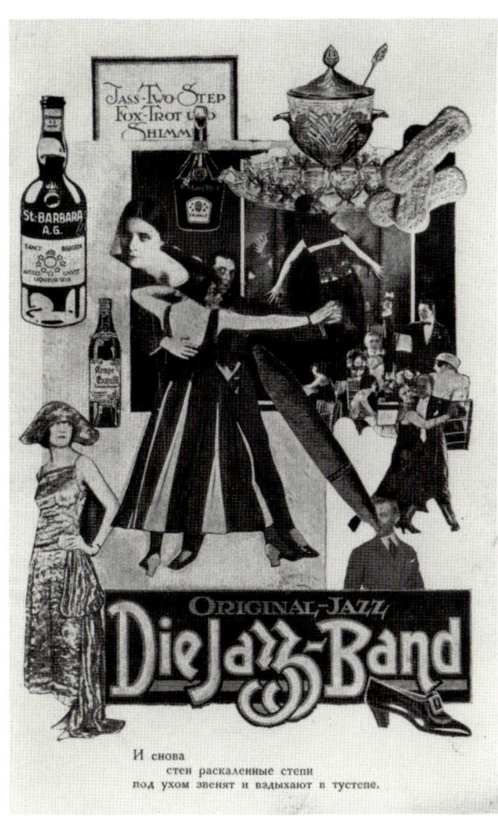

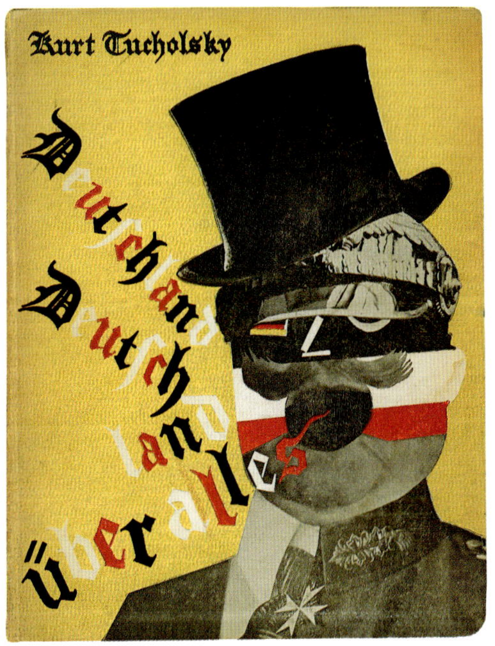

Fig. 28
Aleksander Rodchenko
(Russian, 1891–1956)
Photomontage from:
Vladimir Mayakovski,
Pro Eto. *Moscow: Gos.*
Izd-vo, 1923
Photomechanical
halftone, montage

Fig. 29
John Heartfield
(German, 1891–1968)
Cover of: Kurt Tucholsky,
Deutschland, Deutschland
Über Alles. *Berlin: Neuer*
Deutscher Verlag, 1929
Photomechanical halftone
of photomontage
on cloth binding

observing the American scene, saw the darker aspects of the culture. This image distills the essence of a segregated society, where black citizens ride in the back of the bus.

Arnold Newman is recognized as one of the preeminent portrait photographers of the post-war generation. He is generally credited with introducing the "environmental portrait," where the subject is posed in his or her own home, office, or workplace. The diabolical portrait of Alfried Krupp (figure 32) is one of the few Newman has made that so obviously reveals his personal attitude towards the sitter. During Hitler's Third Reich, Krupp was a high-ranking Nazi whose factory exploited concentration camp labor and literally worked thousands of people to death. Newman deliberately composed and lit this portrait so that Krupp, posed inside one of his factories, is transformed into a malevolent, satanic figure.

The works included in *Language of Light*

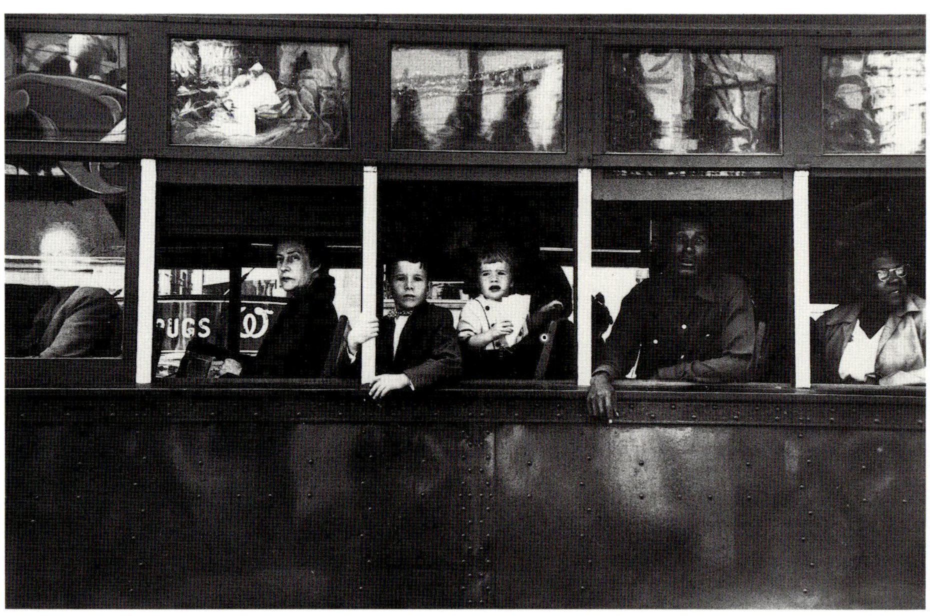

Fig. 31
Robert Frank
(American, b. Switzerland,
1924)
TROLLEY, NEW ORLEANS
ca. 1955–56
From series: The Americans
Gelatin silver print
© Robert Frank

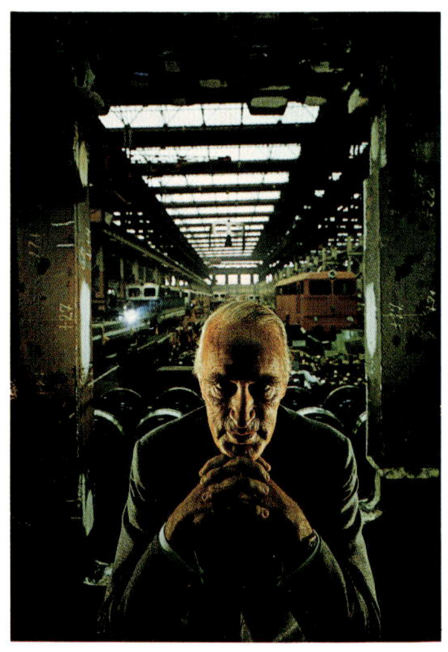

Fig. 32
Arnold Newman
(American, b. 1918)
ALFRIED KRUPP
1963
Dye imbibition (Kodak
Dye Transfer) process
Gift of Lila Acheson
Wallace
© Arnold Newman

were chosen for their aesthetic and historical importance. They are among the many master-works housed in the Museum's collections. The richness and variety of this great collection can be demonstrated with two final comparisons, two pairs of objects that address similar themes and technical challenges.

Garnier's lavish opera house was the ultimate expression of urbane Parisian modernity. Its construction was documented between 1865 and 1870 by the team of Delmaet and Durandelle (figure 33). One albumen print from this series shows the massive steel skeleton of the building under construction. The workmen who pose on the structure are seen by the photographers almost as decorative elements in the bold composition, giving a sense of scale to this unusual archi-tectural study.

The Empire State Building was the sky-scraper that epitomized the power and magnificence of the city in the 1930s. Its construction was docu-mented by Lewis Hine, who composed his pictures to express a very different relationship between the construction worker and the unfinished building (figure 34). The anonymous steelworker is made heroic: elevated above the city, where few have ever been, he calmly surveys his domain. The *Empire State* series was the culmination of Hine's extended study of men and women at work. His images glorify

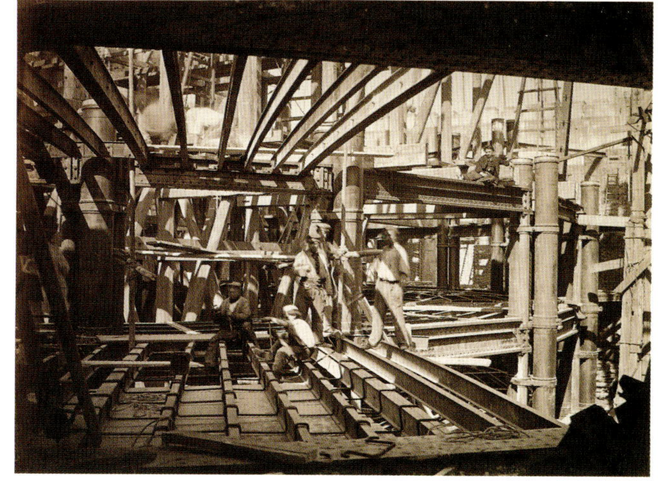

Fig. 33
Delmaet & Durandelle
(French, Hyacinthe
Cèsar Delmaet, 1828–1862;
Clemence Jacob Delmaet,
ca. 1836–ca. 1890;
Louis-Emile Durandelle,
1839–1917)
[Interior view of the
construction of the
Paris Opera House]
ca. 1865–70
Albumen print
Gift of Eastman Kodak
Company, ex-collection
Gabriel Cromer

labor, portraying the worker as dominant over the machines and materials he works with, and over the cities he has built.

Two pieces of apparatus show two different solutions to the design of a panoramic camera. The Lumière Périphote of 1912, with its all-metal body, has an astonishingly contemporary look (figure 35). This advanced camera could cover a 360-degree radius. In operation, a piece of film was positioned around the cylindrical drum. The lens, driven by a clockworks mechanism, moved around the camera, exposing the film. The Globuscope, introduced in 1981, offers a different approach (figure 36). It is a slit-scan panoramic camera that provides an angle of coverage up to 360 degrees, and in fact can make eight and one-half revolutions. It uses 35mm film in standard cassettes. These two cameras show the ingenuity and elegance that distinguish the best in camera design. Such achievements, the triumphs of the medium, are celebrated in the exhibition *Language of Light*.

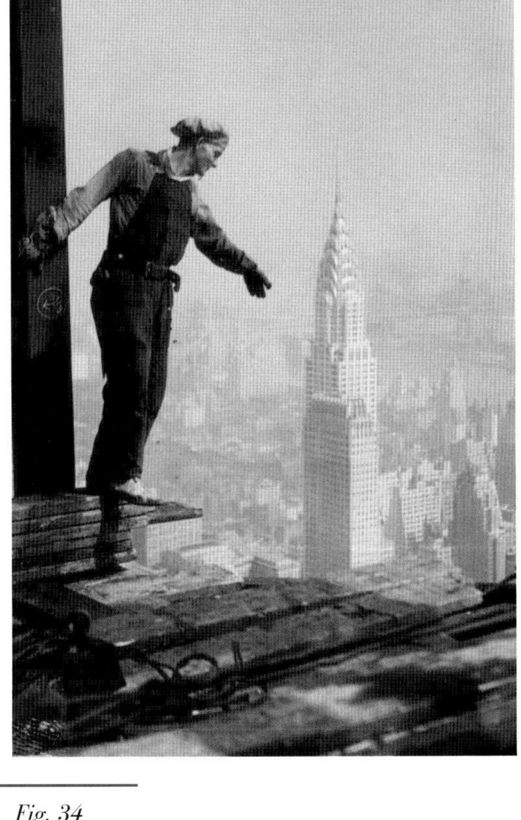

Fig. 34
Lewis W. Hine
(American, 1874–1940)
[Worker, Empire State Building]
ca. 1931
From series: Empire State
Gelatin silver print
Gift of the Photo League, New York, ex-collection Lewis W. Hine

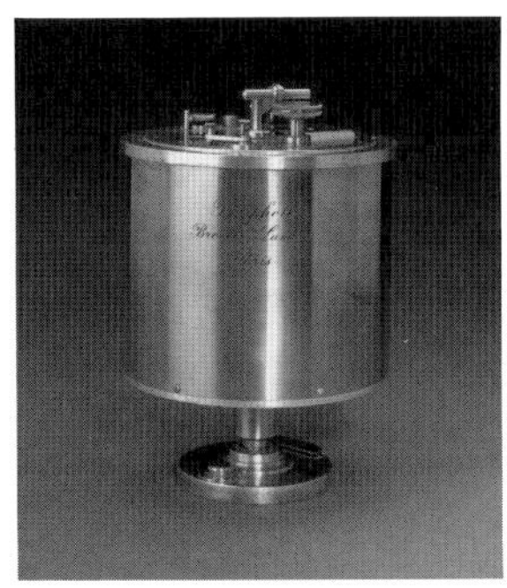 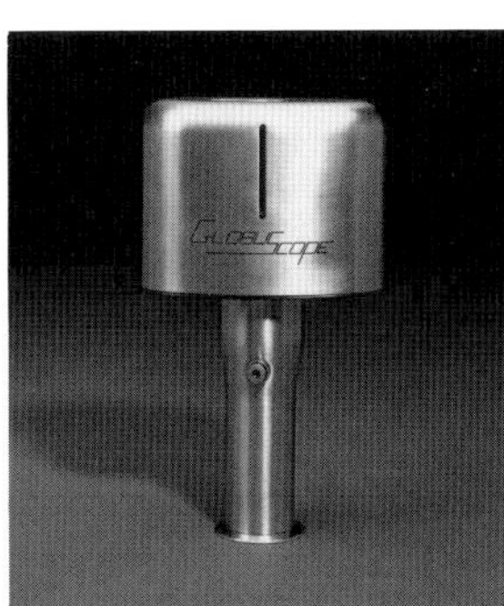

Fig. 35
PÉRIPHOTE PANORAMIC CAMERA
Lumière & Cie, Paris, France
1912

Fig. 36
GLOBUSCOPE
Globuscope Inc., New York, New York
1981
Gift of Globuscope Inc.